THE *Green* SMOOTHIE RECIPE BOOK

DELICIOUS
GREEN SMOOTHIES FOR CLEANSING, DETOX AND RAPID WEIGHT LOSS

Copyright © 2014 Kasia Roberts, RN
All Rights Reserved.

Disclaimer

The information in this book is not to be used as medical advice. The recipes should be used in combination with guidance from your physician. Please consult your physician before beginning any diet. It is especially important for those with diabetes, and those on medications to consult with their physician before starting a diet.

All rights reserved. No part of this publication or the information in it may be quoted from or reproduced in any form by means such as printing, scanning, photocopying or otherwise without prior written permission of the copyright holder.

Effort has been made to ensure that the information in this book is accurate and complete, however, the author and the publisher do not warrant the accuracy of the information, text and graphics contained within the book due to the rapidly changing nature of science, research, known and unknown facts and internet. The Author and the publisher do not hold any responsibility for errors, omissions or contrary interpretation of the subject matter herein. This book is presented solely for motivational and informational purposes only.

Table of Contents

Introduction Green Smoothies 4
Green Smoothies and Weight Loss 6
The Remarkable Fat Burning Nutrient, "Chlorophyll" 6
Cleansing and Detoxifying with Green Smoothies 7
Our Body's Natural Cleansing Organs 7
Drink Green Smoothies for Glowing Skin, Shiny Hair, and Strong Nails 8
Key Nutrients and Their Health Benefits 8
Live Longer with the Anti-Aging Benefits of Green Smoothies 9
The Key Importance of Cellular Regeneration 9
The Role of Anti-Oxidants in Anti-Aging 10
WEIGHT LOSS AND METABOLISM BOOSTERS 11
Tropical Blast Green Smoothie 12
Savory & Spicy Green Smoothie 13
Mint & Ginger Green Smoothie 14
Coconut Pumpkin Green Smoothie 15
Apple Cinnamon Green Smoothie 16
Strawberry-Coconut Green Smoothie 17
LONGEVITY ELIXIRS 18
Basil Grape Elixir 19
Almond Butter & Blueberry Elixir 20
Revitalize & Energize Elixir 21
Cinnamon and Date Elixir 22
Blueberry-Banana Elixir 23
DETOX AND CLEANSING 24
Digestion "Kick-start" Green Smoothie 25
Parsley Flush Green Smoothie 26
Mango-Lemon Delight Green Smoothie 27
Cilantro Detox Green Smoothie 28
Citrus Punch Detox Smoothie 29
RADIANT HAIR, SKIN, AND NAILS 30
Electrolyte Balancer Green Smoothie 31
Skin Revitalizer Green Smoothie 32
Orange-Banana Green Smoothie 33
Sweet Kiwi Green Smoothie 34
Bok Choy Coconut Green Smoothie 35
Conclusion 36

Introduction Green Smoothies

When it comes to revitalizing your health, green smoothies are among the best health alternatives for implementing into your lifestyle. There are vast amounts of people all around the world that have noticed dramatic changes in their health simply by consuming these elixirs of life. As a matter of fact, some who've had chronic illnesses such as eczema, arthritis, or obesity (only to name a few) have noticed remarkable healings.

Ever since processed foods have been introduced to the world, many people have substituted their intake of fruits and vegetables for unhealthy alternatives. This is because most of these foods are artificially flavor-enhanced and very addicting. Through the advent of modern science and technology, scientists have found a way to produce food-grade chemicals that can dramatically change the way food tastes.

Fortunately, with green smoothies, it is much easier to consume a wide variety of vegetables without having to worry about the taste. Simply by adding a few delicious servings of fruits to the smoothie, you won't have to worry about the taste of vegetables. As fruits have a much stronger flavor, when sipping on a green smoothie that's all you'll taste!

In this guide, you'll discover 21 gluten- and dairy-free green smoothie recipes for detox and cleansing, weight loss, radiant hair, skin, and nails and more! With these natural energy-boosting drinks, there's no need to depend on beverages such as coffee, or even worse - energy drinks. Now it's time to introduce a few of the life-changing wellness benefits that you can enjoy by incorporating green smoothies into your arsenal of health alternatives!

Enjoy!
Kasia Roberts, RN

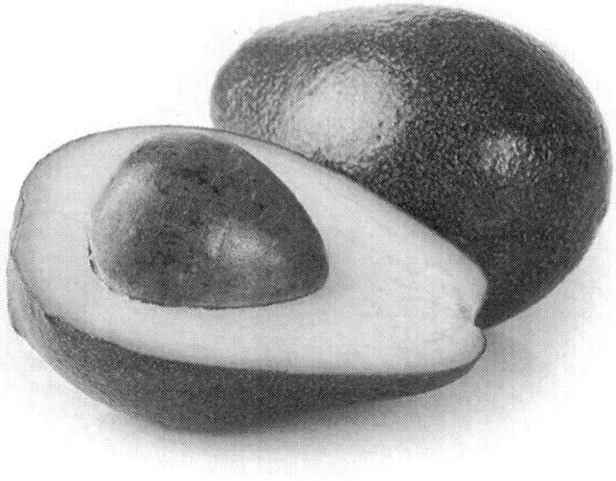

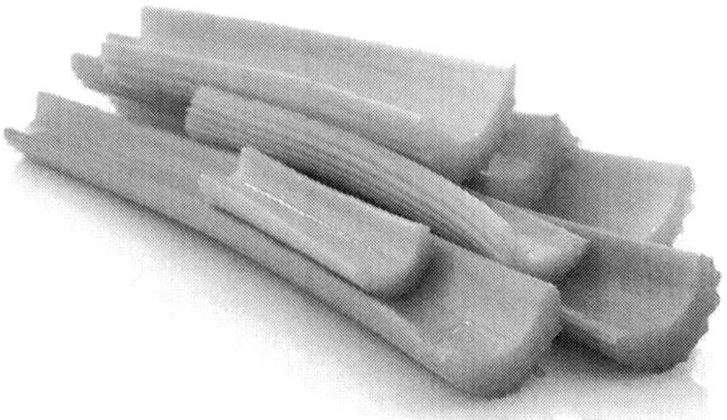

Green Smoothies and Weight Loss

When it comes to the subject of weight loss, there are a lot of controversial 'fad' diets out there, which state, "as long as you stop eating this one particular food product, you'll begin to lose tons of weight." The truth is, in order to lose weight naturally; we must give up processed foods that are high in sugar, fat and sodium and consume a diet rich in organic foods that grow from the earth, such as fresh fruits, vegetables, seeds and various nuts. In this book, I include 21 mouth-watering green smoothie recipes that you'll be able to incorporate into your health plan. Here are a few reasons as to why green smoothies are extremely beneficial for weight loss.

The Remarkable Fat Burning Nutrient, "Chlorophyll."

The primary ingredient that makes green smoothies incredibly healthy and effective for weight loss is found in dark greens. Dark greens are rich in a nutrient known as "chlorophyll". Without this nutrient, leafy vegetables would not be able to develop their green color. In addition, they would lack the ability to synthesize sunlight into energy, which is needed for plant growth. Over the past few decades, more and more people have begun to realize how important it is for weight loss.

Chlorophyll contains a key enzyme, which is known as the "lipolytic enzyme" that enhances the body's natural ability to break down fatty acids. By doing this, it helps your body burn fat, as fatty acids are one of the main culprits for weight-gain. Additionally, these enzymes have the capability to mobilize fatty acids out of fat cells so they can be converted into energy by the body's muscles.

Due to the fact that the consumption of chlorophyll-rich green smoothies can speed up conversion process of converting stored fatty acids into usable energy, it can also help you feel fuller quicker. By feeling fuller, you won't have to eat as much calorie-rich foods in order to maintain adequate energy levels. Here's a tip that can help you buy green vegetables with higher chlorophyll values: the darker the green, the more the chlorophyll in contains.

Cleansing and Detoxifying with Green Smoothies

A popular health trend that is rapidly arising is the use of detox products. People are becoming more aware of the importance of detoxifying and cleansing the body from accumulated toxins. Although it isn't a 'product', green smoothies are one of the most effective detox methods out there!

The fundamental building block for a healthy body is detoxification and cleansing. When toxins accumulate within our bodies, it can become more susceptible to illness and premature aging. One of the best ways to cleanse our system from harmful free radicals and toxins is by consuming green smoothies.

Common benefits of detoxifying with green smoothies include: increased energy, a clearer mind, glowing skin, and a reduced appetite for unhealthy food. Antioxidants are one of the key nutrients that enable green smoothies to be effective cleansers. The key role that antioxidants play is to neutralize toxic chemicals and substances, which are either stored in the body's cells or floating in the bloodstream.

These damaging free radicals are missing an electron, causing them to be unstable. Hence, they must steal an electron from a healthy cell in order to stabilize. However, this isn't completely necessary; antioxidants in green smoothies are able to donate their electron to a free radical so it doesn't have to steal one from a healthy cell.

Our Body's Natural Cleansing Organs

Although our body has various methods of sweeping away these toxins, whether it be help from our liver, immune system, or kidneys, it is still of an utmost importance that we prevent ourselves from relying on these bodily defense mechanisms. If we do, it can put an excessive amount of stress on these organs and may potentially lead to liver disease, autoimmune disorder, or kidney stones. Not only can oxidative stress from toxic overload cause these diseases, but almost every other disease that we know of. Our body's organs were not built to handle a lot of pollutants (which can come from smoking, pollution, alcohol, stress, and processed foods/drinks) so we must do our best to reduce the stress-load by consuming natural foods. By consuming these drinks of green-goodness, rather than focusing on dealing with these toxic materials, our organs can dedicate more energy for healing and cellular regeneration.

Drink Green Smoothies for Glowing Skin, Shiny Hair, and Strong Nails

As many of us know, our skin is also an organ. Inevitably, our skin will lose the glowing look if our body is filled with free radicals and toxins. The basic explanation is: if our system isn't clean enough on the inside, vital organs such as our liver or kidneys won't be able to properly clean toxins from our skin. It is true that our skin is also able to store toxins just like any other organ. To achieve a 'natural glow', we must consume foods that our bodies naturally thrive of, and those are raw fruits and vegetables. Green smoothies are one of the most effective ways to incorporate these vital foods with our daily food intake. Just like all of our body's cells, including our skin cells, antioxidants are able to purge and neutralize toxins. Cleansing and detoxification aren't the only benefits that green smoothies offer; vital nourishment is included as well. Here is a brief list of these nutrients.

Key Nutrients and Their Health Benefits

Silica (celery, cucumber, asparagus, green beans, lettuce) – Being a trace mineral, silica increases the body's ability to heal skin wounds. It can assist with strengthening the skin's connective tissues. Also, silica is commonly known to strengthen hair (by preventing hair-breakage) and nails.

Zinc (ginger, spinach, blackberries, raspberries, Swiss chard) – Zinc can improve the shininess of hair, and prevent brittle nails. Natural-occurring oils are important for the health of our skin, but if too much oil is produced, it can cause acne. Zinc, an important mineral, can help with controlling the oil production.

Vitamin C, E & A (dandelion, kale, collard greens, spinach, cantaloupe) – These crucial vitamins are important for protecting our skin from free radical damage. This damage may be caused by excessive sun exposure, pollution, and chemicals found in beauty products or household cleaners. These key vitamins are crucial for preventing premature hair loss and improving nail strength.

Omega 3 fatty acids (Flax seeds, chia seeds) - Omega 3's are an essential fatty acid (EFA), that are necessary for maintaining skin moisture and flexibility. By having an imbalance of omega 6s to omega 3s, our skin may become inflamed, dry and laden with whiteheads and/or blackheads. When it comes to hair follicles, omega 3s are an effective nourishment alternative; thereby, increasing its strength and health. They can also prevent weak and brittle nails.

Live Longer with the Anti-Aging Benefits of Green Smoothies

A common determining-factor of aging is oxidative stress. What is oxidative stress? It is the stress that our body undergoes when it is subject to free radical damage. Therefore, if we reduce oxidative stress, the slower our body ages.

The Key Importance of Cellular Regeneration

In order to reduce the oxidation of our bodily cells, we must encourage and enhance cellular regeneration. This regeneration process occurs when our body is healing itself. For example, when a toxin that came from an unhealthy meal damages a cell, a new healthy cell will be replicated. However, in order for a new cell to be healthier and stronger than the previous one, we must consume foods that consist of life-giving raw materials. These 'materials' include living enzymes, trace elements, minerals, vitamins, fatty acids and amino acids. These nutrients are particularly abundant in raw fruits and vegetables. Unfortunately, if we don't consume enough of these foods, our body either won't produce a new cell, or the cell that is produced is unhealthy. By incorporating green smoothies into our daily diet, we help facilitate entire organs to be replaced by much healthier cells. This is the main reason as to why there have been countless testimonials around the world whereby people have shared their life-changing stories of overcoming various life-threatening diseases. Did you know that eventually every single cell in our entire body is replaced?

The Role of Anti-Oxidants in Anti-Aging

Not only is cellular regeneration a critical component for slowing the aging process, but neutralizing toxins is as well. By providing our bodies with an abundance of free radical scavengers, otherwise known as antioxidants, we can greatly reduce the amount of cellular damage. The less damage our healthy cells incur, the slower we age. By consuming green smoothies on a regular basis, you will cleanse and remove a lot of these toxins from the body and thereby, prevent healthy cells from being damaged.

Now that we've had an overview of just how effective green smoothies can be for revitalizing our health and well being, here are 21 mouth-watering, energy-boosting recipes. They are very simple to make, yet provide a lot of key nutrients to bring your vitality to the next level. Enjoy!

WEIGHT LOSS

& Metabolism Boosters

Tropical Blast Green Smoothie

When it comes to soothing the GI tract for an optimal digestion, mangoes are highly effective. Not only that, but they are rich in vitamin C, so they can provide a great boost for your body's immune system to fend off bacteria and various pathogens. Pineapples contribute to weight loss because they have a very high water and fiber content. High water/fiber content foods have the ability to make us feel full and contribute to a feeling of satiety. Another reason why pineapples help with weight loss is the fact that they are great for curbing our appetite.

Ingredients
1 cup of pineapple
1 cup of mango
1 cup of banana
¾ cup of spinach
2 cups of fresh coconut water, almond milk, or clean, filtered water.

Directions:
Make sure to thoroughly rinse and clean the spinach in clean water. Dice the pineapple, mango and banana to measure one cup. Add all ingredients to your blender (add spinach last). Blend for 30 seconds to 1 minute, depending on speed setting. Let the ingredients blend until creamy.

Nutritional Information:
Calories: 260
Carbohydrates: 52 g
Protein: 4.5 g
Fat: 3 g

Savory & Spicy Green Smoothie

By adding a bit of jalapeno pepper to your green smoothies, you will be giving it a nutritional punch. A key nutrient found in jalapeno, known as "capsaicin," offers powerful benefits for your metabolism and immune system. Other health benefits includes of increased blood flow, weight loss and energy. This smoothie also serves as a great meal replacement for breakfast; it will keep you full and energized throughout a busy morning. It will also decrease your likelihood of snacking on processed foods with a high fat and sugar content!

Ingredients:
1 whole avocado
1 lemon
1 orange beet (small)
1 cucumber (small)
5 stalks of collards greens
2 drops of vanilla extract
1 inch-thick piece of ginger
½ of a jalapeno pepper

Instructions:
Remove the seeds and skin from the lemon, add to blender. Cut cucumber, orange beet, and collard greens into smaller chunks, then add the collard greens to the blender last. Place the ginger, avocado, jalapeno (with seeds) and clean water in the blender's pitcher last. Blend until the green smoothie reaches your desired consistency.
*Wash the collards, cucumber, and jalapeno thoroughly before adding to blender.

Nutritional Information:
Calories: 396
Carbohydrates: 31 g
Protein: 5 g
Fat: 28 g

Mint & Ginger Green Smoothie

As this recipe includes flax seed, it provides a plentiful amount of heart-healthy omega-3 fatty acids. There is growing evidence that shows that flax seed helps patients who have heart issues, joint pains, diabetes, asthma and even various types of cancers. Omega 3 fatty acids are also great for weight loss, especially for reducing belly fat. According to recent studies, the molecules present in omega 3 fatty acids bind to special receptors on a cell and literally switch on a gene that speeds up your metabolism. Flax seeds also contain an abundance of phytochemicals whereby many of them can help prevent premature aging.

Ingredients:
1 cup of kale (stalk removed)
1 cup of clean filtered water (depending on desired consistency)
1 tsp. ground flax seed (optional)
1 whole pear (seeds removed)
1 ½ inch-thick piece of ginger root
3 leaves of fresh mint

Instructions:
Dice the pear into 2 to 3 pieces, and add it to the blender along with the flax, ginger, mint, and water. Lastly, add the kale after removing the stock (adding the kale first will make it difficult to blend.)
*Remember to wash the kale, pear, mint, and ginger before adding to blender.

Nutritional Information:
Calories: 142
Carbohydrates: 28 g
Protein: 3 g
Fat: 2 g

Coconut Pumpkin Green Smoothie

Although it isn't commonly used in green smoothies, pumpkin puree really does make them taste delectable, almost just like a pumpkin pie. With this serving-size of pumpkin puree, you will be getting about 6 times the daily recommended amount of Vitamin A. This vitamin is essential for the health of your eyes, lungs, heart and kidneys.
Coconut oil is great for facilitating weight loss. It's rich in medium chain triglycerides (MCFAs), which increases the liver's rate of metabolism by up to 30 percent, according to various research studies.

Ingredients:
2/3 cup of pumpkin puree
1 1/2 tbsp. coconut oil
1 cup almond milk, coconut water (or clean water)
1 medium-sized pear
1 cup spinach
1 tbsp. Avocado (optional)
1 cup red seedless grapes

Instructions:
First thoroughly wash spinach, grapes, and the pear in water with a bit of vinegar (vinegar helps to clean more impurities from the produce).
Add the tbsp. of avocado, grapes, pear, almond milk (or coconut water), coconut oil, water, and then blend. While blending, slowly add the pumpkin puree and then the lettuce. Allow it to blend until it reached your desired texture.

Nutritional Information:
Calories: 255
Carbohydrates: 42 g
Protein: 6 g
Fat: 7 g

Apple Cinnamon Green Smoothie

The key ingredient in this green smoothie, cinnamon, is well known for its ability to boost the body's metabolism. By doing so, losing weight is much easier as our system is able to convert food into useable energy more efficiently, leading to less fat storage. Additionally, with its anti-bacterial and anti-fungal properties, it is able to fend off pathogens and other strains of bacteria that can lead to sickness.

Ingredients:
2 medium apples (peeled and cored)
½ tsp. cinnamon (grounded)
1 medium banana
1½ cups of romaine Lettuce
1 cup of clean, filtered water

Instructions:
Wash and soak the apples and romaine in a bowl with water and vinegar (for enhanced cleaning effects).
Dice the apples and romaine. Add the apple chunks, cinnamon, banana and water to the blender. After blending for about 5 seconds, then add the romaine and allow it to mix until the smoothie reaches your desired consistency.

Nutritional Information:
Calories: 192
Carbohydrates: 43 g
Protein: 3 g
Fat: 2 g

Strawberry-Coconut Green Smoothie

Omega-3 fatty acids are critical for the overall health and functionality of our brain, bodily cells and hormones. If your goal is to ensure long-term health, then you should make it a goal to consume either hemp or Chia seeds each and every day. Lemons are amazing liver detoxifiers and also alkalize our body. They may seem acidic based on taste but in the process of being metabolized by the body, they actually alkalize our bodily fluids and tissues. Maintaining the health of the liver is also imperative to the body's ability to digest and burn fat, since the liver is one of the organs responsible for these functions.

Ingredients:
1 cup of strawberries
1/2 lemon (without skin)
2 kale leaves (without stem)
1 cup of coconut water
1.5 tbsp. coconut oil
1 tbsp. hemp seeds

Instructions:
First allow the strawberries and kale to soak in a bowl of water with a dash of vinegar (for better cleaning). Then add the coconut oil, coconut water, hemp seeds, lemon, and strawberries to the blender. After chopping the kale into smaller pieces, add it last. Blend until your desired consistency.

Nutritional Information:
Calories: 237
Carbohydrates: 31 g
Protein: 8 g
Fat: 9 g

LONGEVITY Elixirs

Basil Grape Elixir

This green smoothie elixir is perfect for preventing oxidative stress and reducing inflammation. By adding basil to the mix, it provides your body's cells with added protection against DNA and RNA damage, which is caused by oxidative stress. In addition, basil has received a lot of attention for its ability to enhance cardiovascular health. One of the key steps for preventing illness is by reducing inflammation, and best of all, this green smoothie is capable of neutralizing inflammation.

Ingredients:
5 leaves freshly picked basil
3 romaine lettuce leaves
1 cup of fresh red grapes
2 celery sticks
½ lemon, unpeeled and deseeded
1 cup of clean, filtered water

Instructions:
First, rinse and wash the grapes, celery, basil and lettuce. Tip: Soak fruit and vegetables in water with a bit of vinegar, this will ensure they are thoroughly cleaned and free of debris and dirt. After washing, add the fresh grapes, basil and lemon to the pitcher. Dice the celery and romaine, and add it with the others. Add water and blend well or until desired consistency.

Nutritional Information:
Calories: 150
Carbohydrates: 30 g
Protein: 3 g
Fat: 2 g

Almond Butter & Blueberry Elixir

If you're craving a green smoothie that has a delicious creamy and "almondy" flavor, you have to try adding almond butter. Almond butter is primarily composed of healthy monounsaturated fats, and it has been shown that these are effective for lowing levels of cholesterol and high blood pressure. Additionally, it is a great source of various anti-oxidants such as flavonoids and vitamin E, which are important for the prevention of premature aging.

Ingredients:
1 cup almond milk (or clean water)
1 tbsp. almond butter
1 cup of fresh blueberries
2 cups spinach

Instructions:
After cleaning the blueberries and spinach with water, add them to the blender along with the almond butter and milk. Blend until desired consistency and enjoy.

Nutritional Information:
Calories: 212
Carbohydrates: 21 g
Protein: 5 g
Fat: 12 g

Revitalize & Energize Elixir

Since this green smoothie is primarily composed of carbohydrates that are easy-to-digest, it will provide you with sustained energy throughout the day. Thanks to the spinach and chia seeds, it's abundant in minerals such as sodium and potassium.
This green smoothie can enhance your cells' energy-production capabilities. Coconut water is an excellent source of electrolytes, such as potassium, essential for hydration. Blueberries are rich in antioxidants and help battle body fat while decreasing the risk of cardiovascular disease and diabetes.

Ingredients:
1 ½ inch-thick piece of ginger root
1 cup of spinach
1 cup of coconut water
1 whole pear (peeled and cored)
1 tbsp. of hemp seeds
1 cup of blueberries

Instructions:
Rinse and wash the ginger, spinach, pear and blueberries with water and a tbsp. of vinegar.
First add the blueberries, hemp seeds, pear, coconut water and ginger and then blend. After about 5-10 seconds, add the spinach and allow to blend thoroughly until it reaches your desired consistency.

Nutritional Information:
Calories: 252
Carbohydrates: 39 g
Protein: 6 g
Fat: 8 g

Cinnamon and Date Elixir

Dates are a nutrient-packed dry fruit that are always perfect for adding sweetness to your smoothies. They are rich in a wide array of minerals, including of potassium, iron, manganese, magnesium and calcium. Additionally, by being a high source of soluble fiber, they will help keep your GI tract happy. A perfect boost of nutrients and flavor!

Kale is a detoxifying, cancer-fighting superfood. It's packed with fiber and sulfur, both great for detoxification and overall liver health. Powerful antioxidants, such as carotenoids and flavonoids, protect against cancers, as does the high level of vitamin K. Kale is also rich in vitamins A and C, calcium, and contains more iron per calorie than beef.

Ingredients:
1 apple (any kind)
3 Medjool dates (pits removed)
2 kale leaves (stems removed)
1 tsp. of cinnamon powder
1 tbsp. of hemp or chia seeds
1 cup of clean water

Instructions:
After soaking the kale and apple in a bowl of water for cleaning, dice both of them into smaller pieces. To the blender, add dates, apple chunks, cinnamon, hemp/chia and water. Make sure to add the kale last. Then blend for 1 minute or more if required to reach your preferred consistency.

Nutritional Information:
Calories: 260
Carbohydrates: 38 g
Protein: 9 g
Fat: 8 g

Blueberry-Banana Elixir

By adding blueberries to your smoothies, you'll be taking the antioxidant value to a whole new level. Additionally, as kale is abundant in iron, you'll be increasing your blood's efficiency for transporting oxygen and nutrients to your bodily cells. When you get the chance, add kale to your smoothies!

Ingredients:
1 banana
2 cups of blueberries
2 leaves kale (without stems)
1.5 inch-thick piece of ginger root
1 tbsp. of chia seeds
2 cups coconut water (or clean water)

Instructions:
First wash and rinse the kale, ginger and blueberries and then add them to the blender except the kale. Add the banana, chia seeds and coconut water. Add the kale last and blend until it reaches your desired consistency.

Nutritional Information:
Calories: 292
Carbohydrates: 56 g
Protein: 9 g
Fat: 8 g

DETOX
& Cleansing

Digestion "Kickstart" Green Smoothie

The three key ingredients in this smoothie that can "kickstart" your digestion are pineapple, ginger and lime. Firstly, pineapple has a certain enzyme otherwise known as bromelain, where it is beneficial for enhancing the digestive flow. Ginger is particularly good for promoting the production of good bacteria in the GI tract, and it helps to get rid of constipation-causing bad bacteria. As for lime, it is a great overall detoxification ability to eliminate unwanted pathogens and parasites from the colon.

Ingredients:
1 cup of fresh pineapple
1 lime, unpeeled
2 inch-thick piece of ginger root
½ bunch of parsley
1 cup of romaine lettuce
½ medium-sized cucumber
1 cup of filtered water or coconut water

Instructions:
After thoroughly rinsing the parsley, romaine and cucumber, add them to the blender except the romaine. Also add the ginger, coconut water, pineapple, lime, and the lettuce lastly. Blend until it reaches your desired consistency.

Nutritional Information:
Calories: 166
Carbohydrates: 34 g
Protein: 3 g
Fat: 2 g

Parsley Flush Green Smoothie

If you're looking to detoxify and flush your kidneys, this is a green smoothie that you should try out. Being uncommonly talked about, parsley is a super-healthy herb that is particularly good for removing toxic wastes, which may lead to kidney stones. In addition, it's also great for the relief of constipation, asthma and high blood pressure, to only name a few.

Ingredients:
1/2 bunch of fresh parsley
1-inch piece ginger root
1 medium banana
1 stick of celery
1 cup of spinach
1 whole lime
1 cup of coconut water or clean water

Instructions:
In a bowl, add the parsley, spinach, celery and ginger to allow them to soak until they are completely removed of impurities. Then add ginger, celery, lime, coconut water, parsley and banana to the blender (adding the spinach last). Now blend all of the ingredients until they reach your desired smoothness and consistency.

Nutritional Information:
Calories: 82
Carbohydrates: 24 g
Protein: 4 g
Fat: 2 g

Mango-Lemon Delight Green Smoothie

One of the most effective fruits for aiding digestion are mangoes. They have a wide array of enzymes that are good for soothing the digestive walls to release toxic build-up. Not only that, but they are abundant in vitamins such as A and C, which can help to protect the body from free-radical damage and premature aging.

Ingredients:
1 cup of fresh mango
2 cups of green leaf or romaine lettuce
1 lime (peeled, seeds removed)
⅓ bunch of cilantro
1 tbsp. of hemp seeds
1 cup of filtered water

Instructions:
After adding some water and a bit of vinegar (for enhancing cleaning effects) to a large mixing bowl, allow the lettuce and cilantro to rinse until they are removed of impurities. Then in the blender, add the water, lime, hemp seeds, mango, cilantro and lettuce (make sure the lettuce is added last) and then blend until it is mixed enough to reach your desired consistency.

Nutritional Information:
Calories: 211
Carbohydrates: 29 g
Protein: 8 g
Fat: 7 g

Cilantro Detox Green Smoothie

One of the best herbs for removing heavy metals, especially mercury, from the body is cilantro. Cilantro is an herb that you should add to your green smoothie recipes regularly if you have amalgam fillings, as these fillings are made up of about 50% mercury. Cilantro is also referred to as a heavy metal "chelator." The definition of chelator is quite specific, denoting a food or supplement that is capable of removing heavy metals, such as mercury, from the body. Along with the pineapple, your digestion will be greatly cleansed by consuming this green smoothie. Thus, it is an all-round great smoothie recipe for detoxification.

Ingredients:
1 cup of coconut water or filtered water
1 cup of fresh pineapple
½ of a bunch of cilantro
1 celery rib, chopped
1 cup of chopped romaine lettuce

Instructions:
In a large mixing bowl, add the cilantro, celery and romaine along with water and a tablespoon of vinegar (to increase the cleaning effect). Then in the blender's pitcher, add the coconut water, pineapple, cilantro, celery and romaine (adding the lettuce last), blend until it's smooth enough to be free of fibrous chunks.

Nutritional Information:
Calories: 147
Carbohydrates: 26 g
Protein: 4 g
Fat: 3 g

Citrus Punch Detox Smoothie

When it comes to ridding your body of unwanted mucus, no other family of fruit can be quite as effective as citrus fruits. By detoxifying from mucus, your body will be able to better absorb crucial nutrients.

Ingredients:
2 kale leaves (without stems)
½ cup of chopped cilantro
1 lime
1 large-sized banana
½ red grapefruit
2 small oranges
1 lemon
1 to 2 cups of filtered water (depending on your desired consistency.)

Instructions:
Thoroughly wash the cilantro and kale before preparing it for your blender. Peel the skin and deseed the lemon, lime, oranges and grapefruit, and then add them to the blender. Add the banana. Thoroughly wash the cilantro and kale leaves, and then place them in the blender along with the clean water. Blend until desired consistency.

Nutritional Information:
Calories: 226
Carbohydrates: 48 g
Protein: 4 g
Fat: 2 g

RADIANT HAIR
Skin & Nails

Electrolyte Balancer Green Smoothie

When it comes enhancing the balance of your body's electrolytes, coconut milk and celery are noticeably advantageous. Also, by adding pineapple, not only can this smoothie help your body fend off various strains of bacteria and infections, it can also provide quality nourishment for your hair and skin.

Ingredients:
2 cups of fresh pineapple
2 fresh celery ribs, chopped
1 cup of spinach
1 lime (without skin and seeds)
2 cups of coconut milk

Instructions:
Before adding the celery and spinach to the blender, first thoroughly soak & rinse them with water to clean them of all unwanted impurities. Then in the blender's pitcher, add the chopped pineapple chunks, celery, lime, coconut milk and spinach; allow all of the fresh ingredients to blend until it reaches a creamy smooth texture.

Nutritional Information:
Calories: 231
Carbohydrates: 34 g
Protein: 8 g
Fat: 7 g

Skin Revitalizer Green Smoothie

When it comes to protecting the skin from damage caused by free radicals, spinach, cucumbers, and blueberries are among the most beneficial foods. They are particularly abundant in a nutrient that's known as silica, which helps the skin achieve a glowing look. If your goal is to hydrate and enhance the health of your skin, this green smoothie recipe is great for you!

Ingredients:
2 inch-thick piece of ginger root
1 cup of spinach
½ bunch of parsley
½ medium-sized cucumber
1 banana
½ cup of blueberries
1 cup of filtered water, (or coconut water)

Instructions:
Prior to blending the blueberries, cucumber, spinach and parsley, first soak them in a large mixing bowl with clean water and a dash of vinegar (for added cleaning effects). Afterwards, place them in the blender's pitcher along with the banana, coconut water and ginger. Blend it until completely smooth.

Nutritional Information:
Calories: 211
Carbohydrates: 41 g
Protein: 5 g
Fat: 3 g

Orange-Banana Green Smoothie

The best way, to get nutrition from oranges is to eat them whole or by blending or juicing them yourself. Store-bought orange juice has been sitting on the shelves for days, or even worse, for weeks. Many orange juice products consist of only water and synthetic orange flavoring (with no nutrition at all!). By using freshly blended or juiced oranges, you are getting a higher value of vitamin A & C, which is crucial for your body to fend off toxins, pathogens, and bacteria. Remember: When it comes to fruits and vegetables, fresh is always best!

Ingredients:
1 cup spinach
1 large banana
2 celery ribs
2 oranges (peeled)
1 coconut water or filtered water

Instructions:
Allow the spinach and celery to soak in water to remove any impurities. Then add oranges, celery, banana and coconut water to the blender. Make sure to add the spinach last, and allow the mix to blend until it is creamy enough for your preference.

Nutritional Information:
Calories: 295
Carbohydrates: 62 g
Protein: 5 g
Fat: 3 g

Sweet Kiwi Green Smoothie

Kiwis contain high levels of omega 3 fatty acids, unlike most other fruits. In addition, they are a great source of potassium and vitamin C. Recent research has found that kiwis are especially effective for preventing cellular oxidation. Cucumbers contain silica, a trace mineral that increases the body's ability to heal skin wounds. It can also assist with strengthening the skin's connective tissues.

Ingredients:
2 leaves kale (without stems)
1 medium cucumber (peeled)
2 kiwis (without skin)
2 Medjool date (pitted)
1 cup of coconut water (or clean water)

Instructions:
First wash the kale and cucumber. Dice both and add the cucumber to the blender, along with the kiwis, dates and coconut water. Add the kale last while blending. Allow the mixture of fruits and vegetables to blend until they reach your desired consistency.

Nutritional Information:
Calories: 178
Carbohydrates: 36 g
Protein: 4 g
Fat: 2 g

Bok Choy Coconut Green Smoothie

There are many people who are passionate about making smoothies with Bok Choy as an ingredient. One main reason as to why you should consider adding it to your smoothie is because it is extremely abundant in calcium. Calcium is crucial for the health of our teeth and bones. In addition, it also plays an important role in enhancing muscle contraction and nerve function.

Ingredients:
1 cup of Pineapple
1 cup of coconut water
1 head of Bok Choy
1 cup of Spinach
1 piece ginger root (1 to 1.5 inch-thick)
1 tbsp. Hemp or Chia Seeds

Instructions:
Prepare the pineapple by cutting it into small pieces to measure one cup, and then add it to the blender. Pour the coconut water into the pitcher. Afterwards, cut the Bok Choy into small pieces, and add it with the others, including the ginger root, hemp/chia seeds and spinach. Blend until it reaches your desired consistency.

Nutritional Information:
Calories: 200
Carbohydrates: 38 g
Protein: 5 g
Fat: 7 g

Conclusion

On a global basis, the consumption of green smoothies is gaining popularity at an exceptional speed. As our lives are becoming busier and busier, the time saving benefits that these elixirs provide are phenomenal. No longer are you required to sit at a kitchen table, and spend 20 to 30 minutes to chow down on a salad. By making a green smoothie, you can simply pour it in a sealable container and then take it on the go with you.
Not only are these nutrient-rich drinks convenient, they are also life-changing. People of all walks of life are noticing dramatic improvements from the simplest health complications to the most complex. Green smoothies allow us to consume all of the plant-based goodness without having to sacrifice taste. Consuming a salad is unthinkable by many; however, as the taste of fruits always overtakes the vegetable bitterness when blended into a smoothie, it's simple to get the best of both worlds.
When it comes to health benefits, there are many of them – ranging from weight loss all the way to beautification. Green smoothies are abundant in chlorophyll, which can help aid the metabolism's fat burning process and anti-oxidants which can reduce oxidative stress thereby allowing anyone to live a longer, more energetic life. And it doesn't stop there, with all of the vital nutrients that they provide; green smoothies can enhance the shininess of hair, strengthen the nails and teeth, and even amplify the skin's glow. The journey of eating enough fruits and vegetables need not be stressful when incorporating the green smoothie lifestyle.
By utilizing the included pre-made recipes, thinking about what to blend for a succulent smoothie can be brought down to a tee. I have conducted all of the hard work so you won't have to go through the rigmarole of guesswork. Simply make it a priority to bring your level of health to new heights, utilize the tools that have been provided, and make a new grocery-shopping list for your green smoothies.

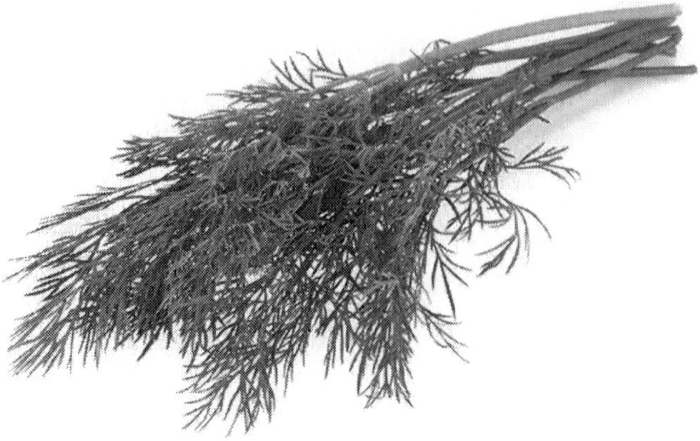

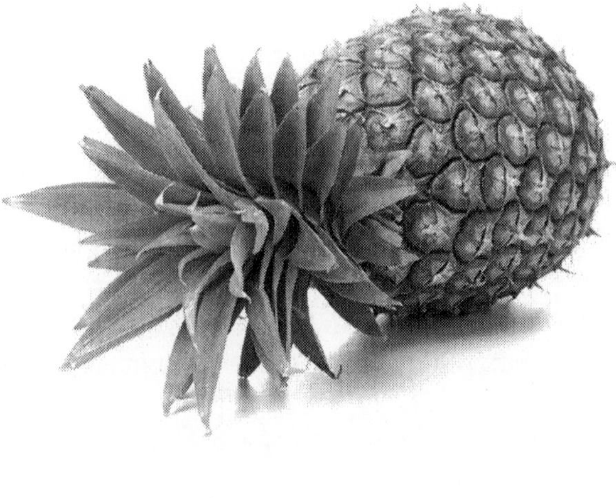

Thank You

Thank you for purchasing The Green Smoothie Recipe Book! If you have enjoyed this book please be sure to check out
" THE SUPERFOOD SMOOTHIE RECIPE BOOK: SUPER-NUTRITIOUS HIGH-PROTEIN SMOOTHIES TO LOSE WEIGHT, BOOST METABOLISM AND INCREASE ENERGY."
by Kasia Roberts, RN

Printed in Great Britain
by Amazon.co.uk, Ltd.,
Marston Gate.